The Orange Family

Hello...yel..low!

I introduce you to Willie, the yellow wiggly worm who lives on the beach where everything is yellow.

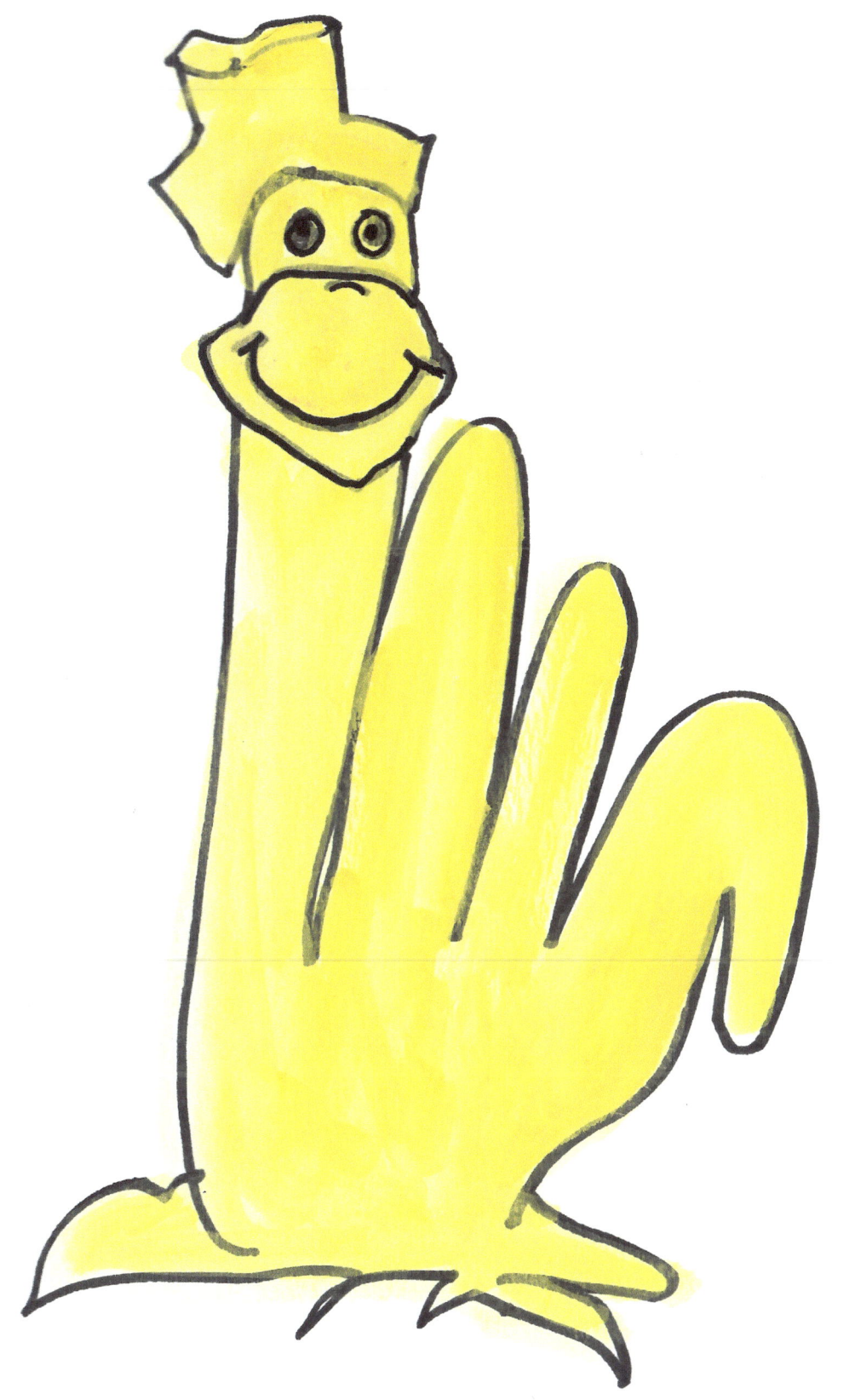

Willie lives outside all the time. He crawls along the beaches near the water and sometimes sleeps under a rock or some tall grasses. He loves the sunshine! Why not? The big sun is bright yellow just like him...and when it shines down the lagoon, the water, the sand , the grasses, all shimmer with a golden light.

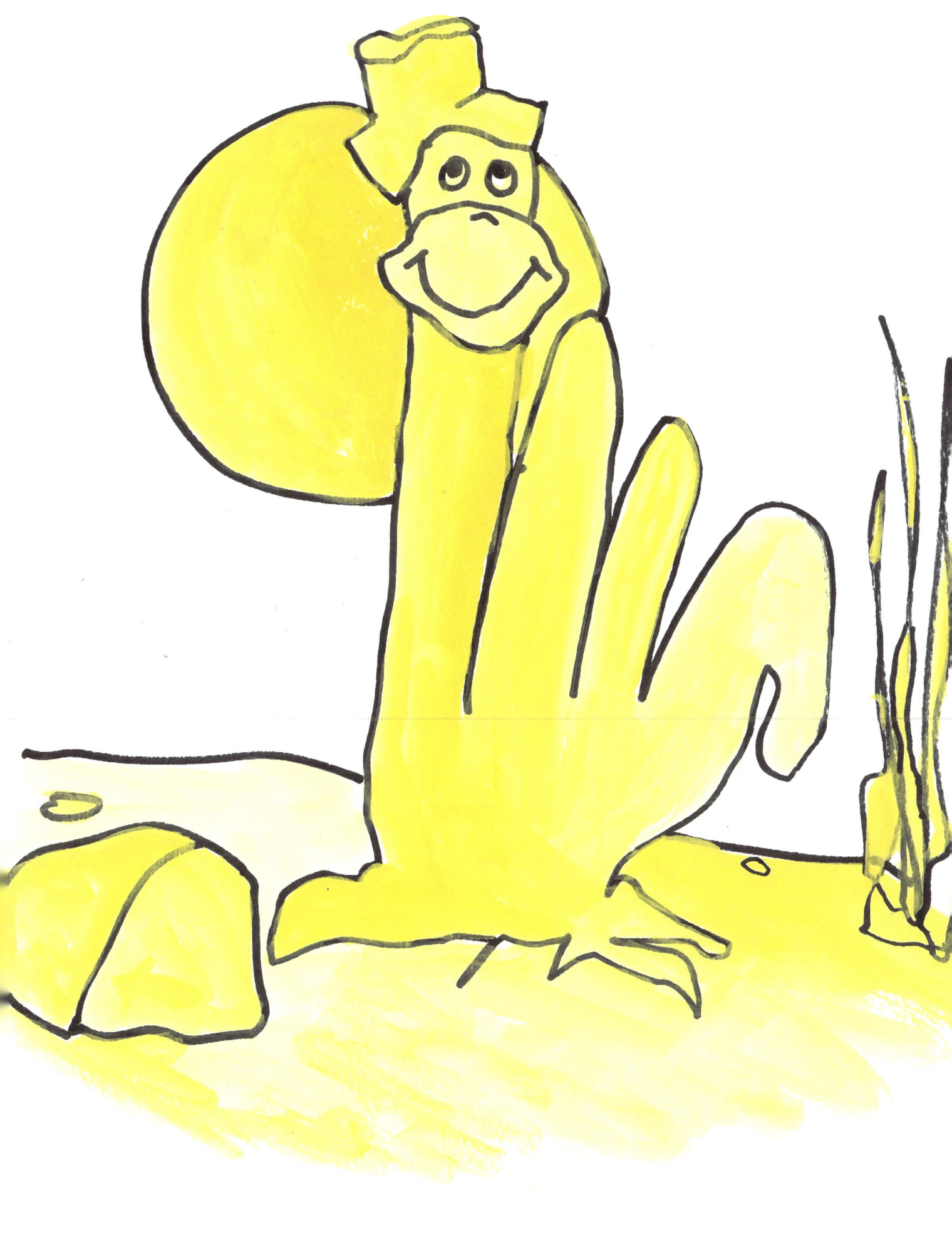

One day as Willie was crawling the beach he was startled by something red. Yes, red not yellow.

It was a red snail!

Meet Rosie, the beautiful red snail. She too loved the beach but until today her whole world was red. She hung out in her shell which was red and her favorite flower was a rose... a red rose.

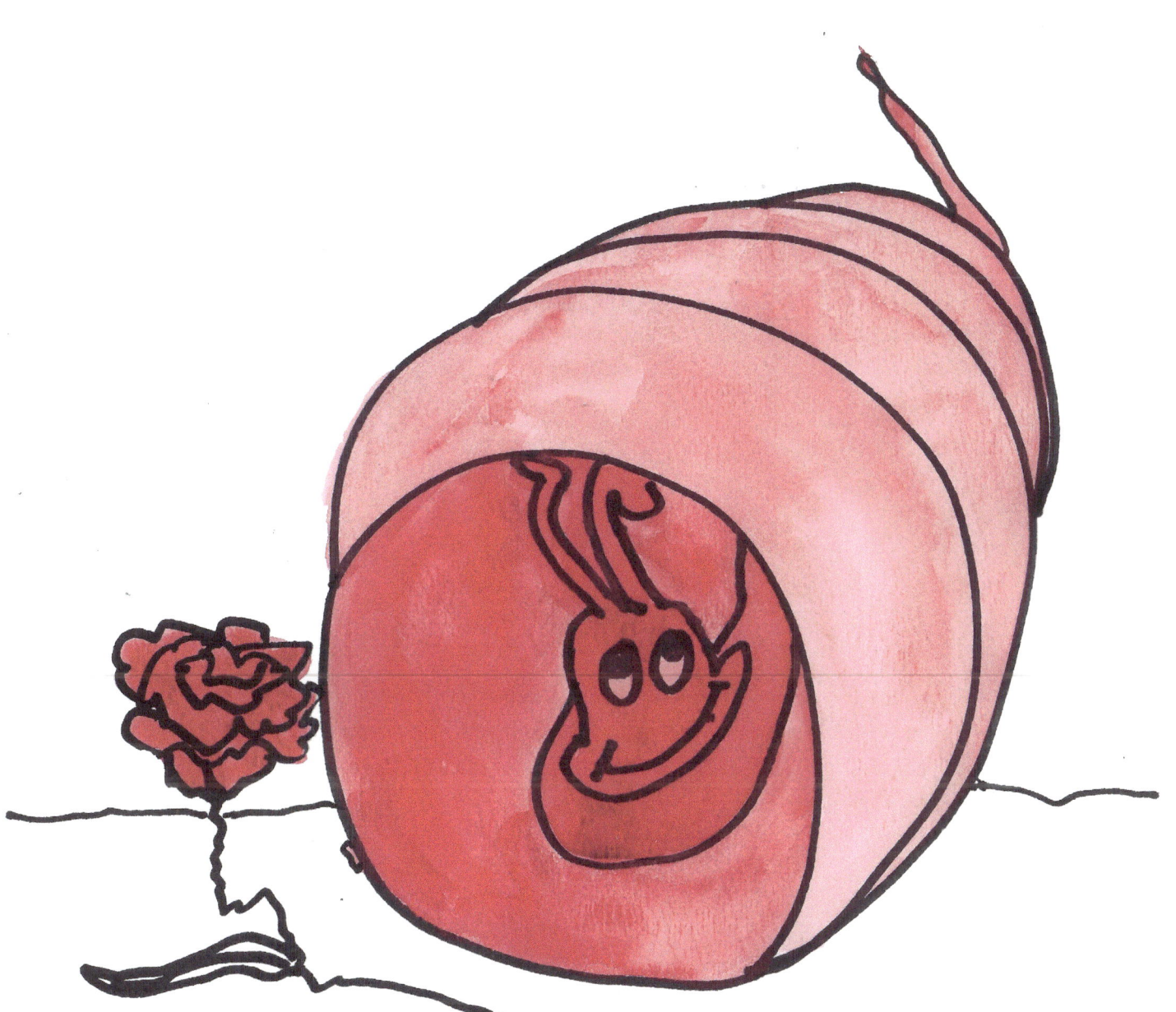

Rosie was very shy but today she was so excited to meet someone else on the beach that she came out of her shell...Willie had that effect on her.

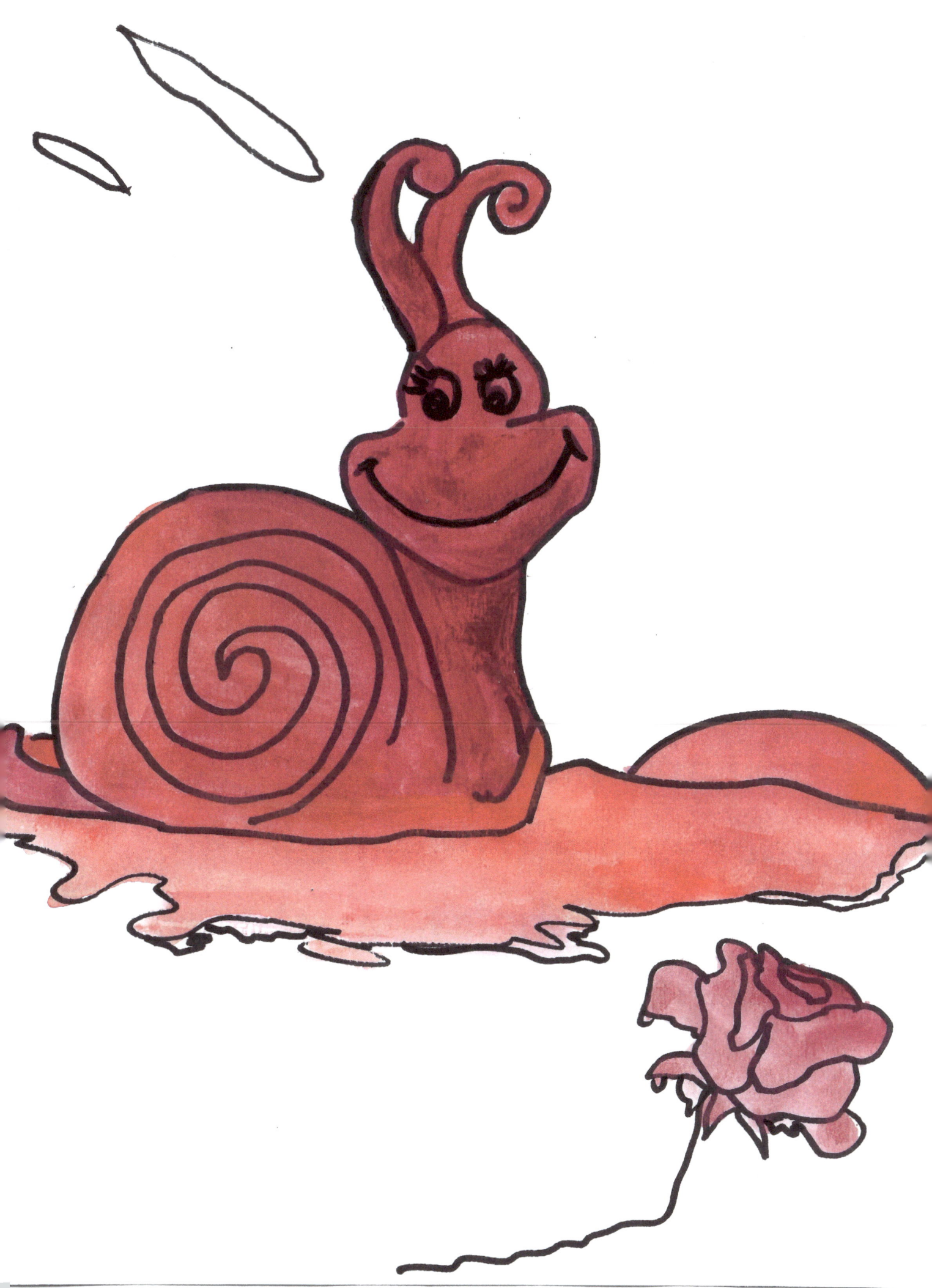

Rosie decided to join Willie . The golden glow of the sea as the sun settled down beyond the horizon. How beautiful! They became close friends and their friendship turned into a very strong love. Inside of each of them their hearts turned a brilliant red...if they were quiet enough they could hear the beating of their hearts! They mixed!

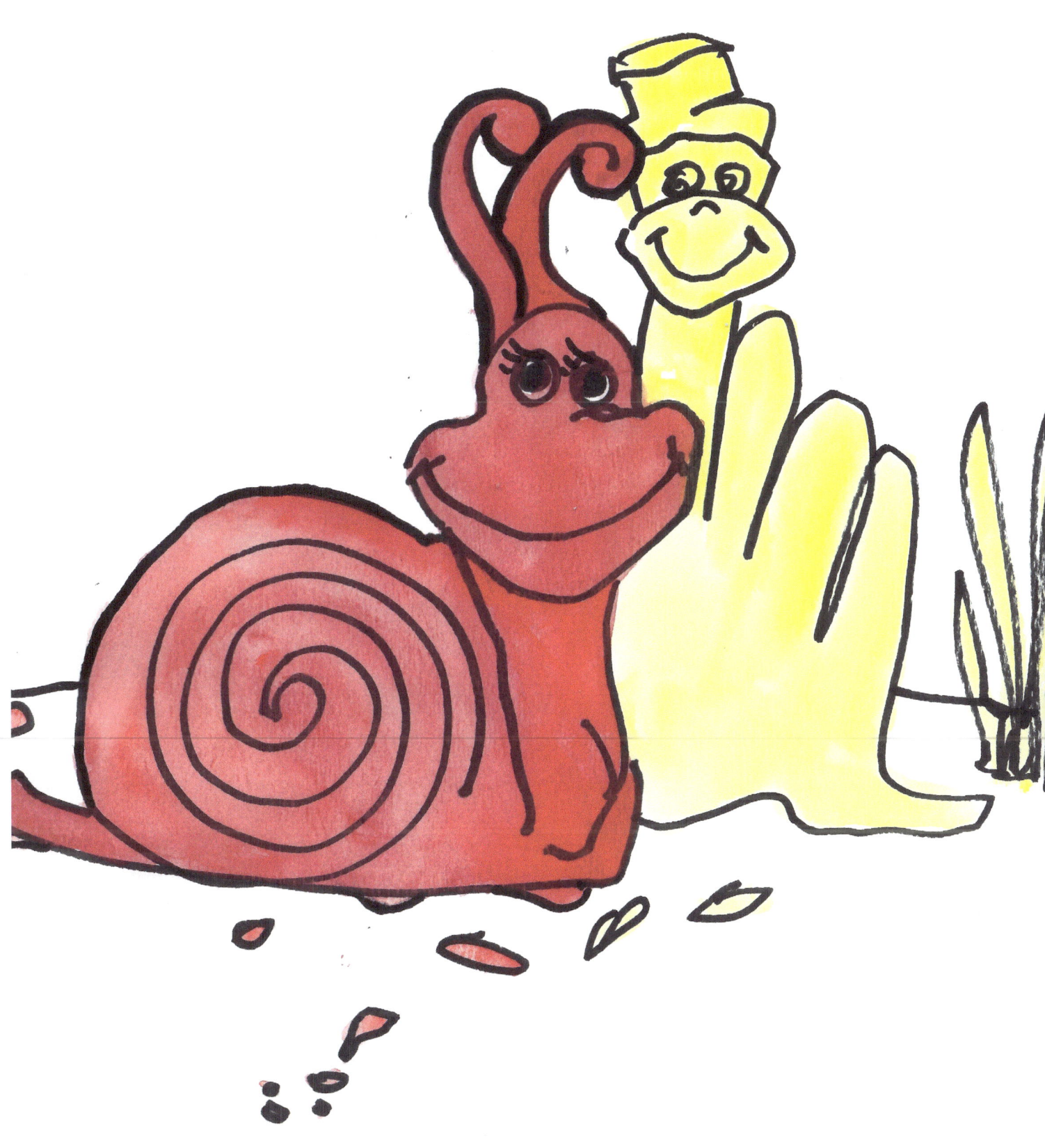

And lo and behold a new creature emerged on the beach...a sort of perfect combination of Willie, the wiggly worm, and Rosie the red snail...but wait...he was not red nor yellow...or was he a perfect amount of each? A perfect mix of red and yellow!

He was orange!

They named him Sammy. Where had they seen that color before?

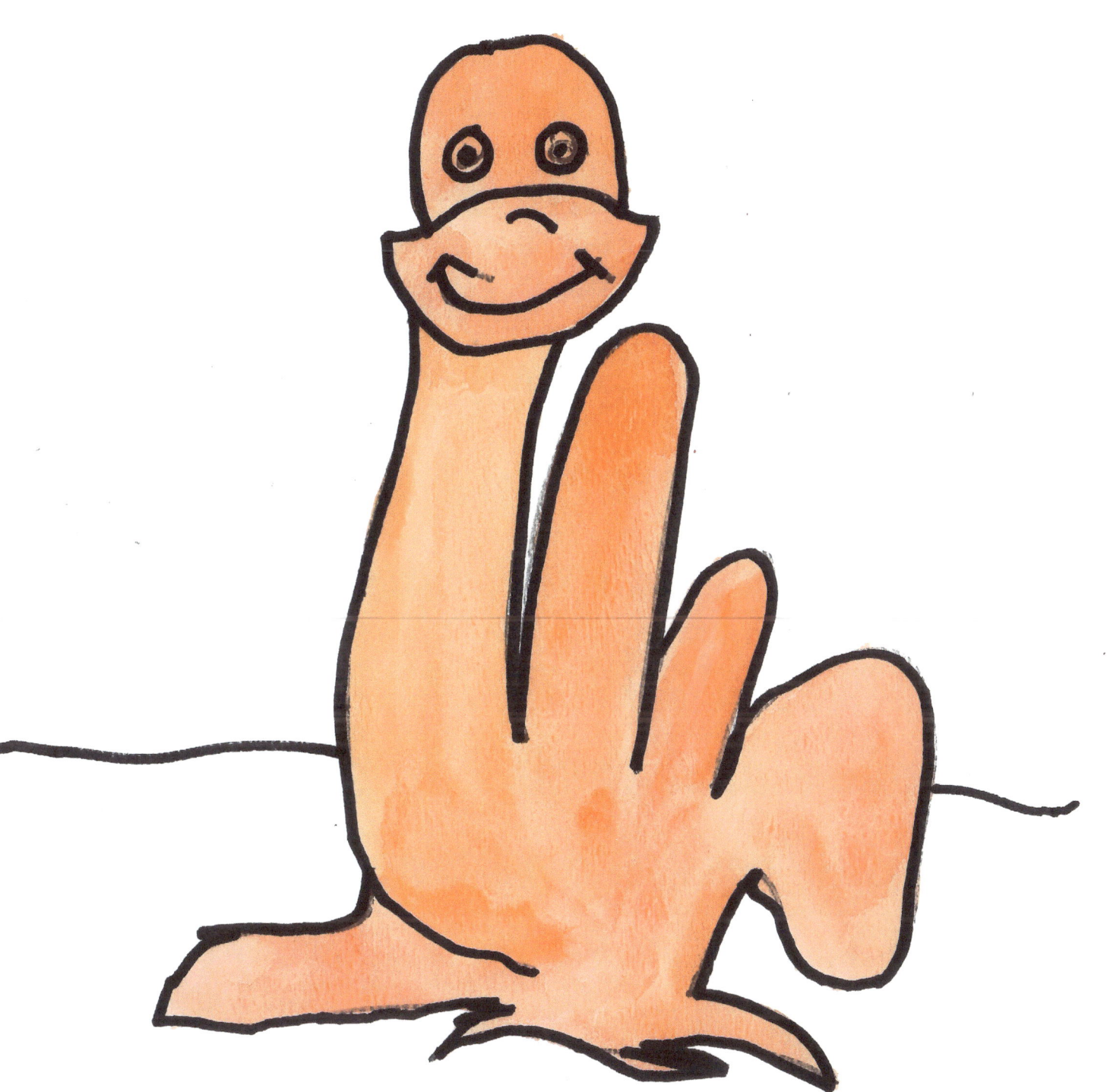

That evening the three strolled the beach and they started noticing the colors changing on the sand and the sea and in the sky. First the bright yellow sun like Willie and then a few moments later, the sky lit up in a bright red like Rosie. The sea still reflected the yellow and the red and then a big bright orange broke out from the sun as it headed down toward the horizon.

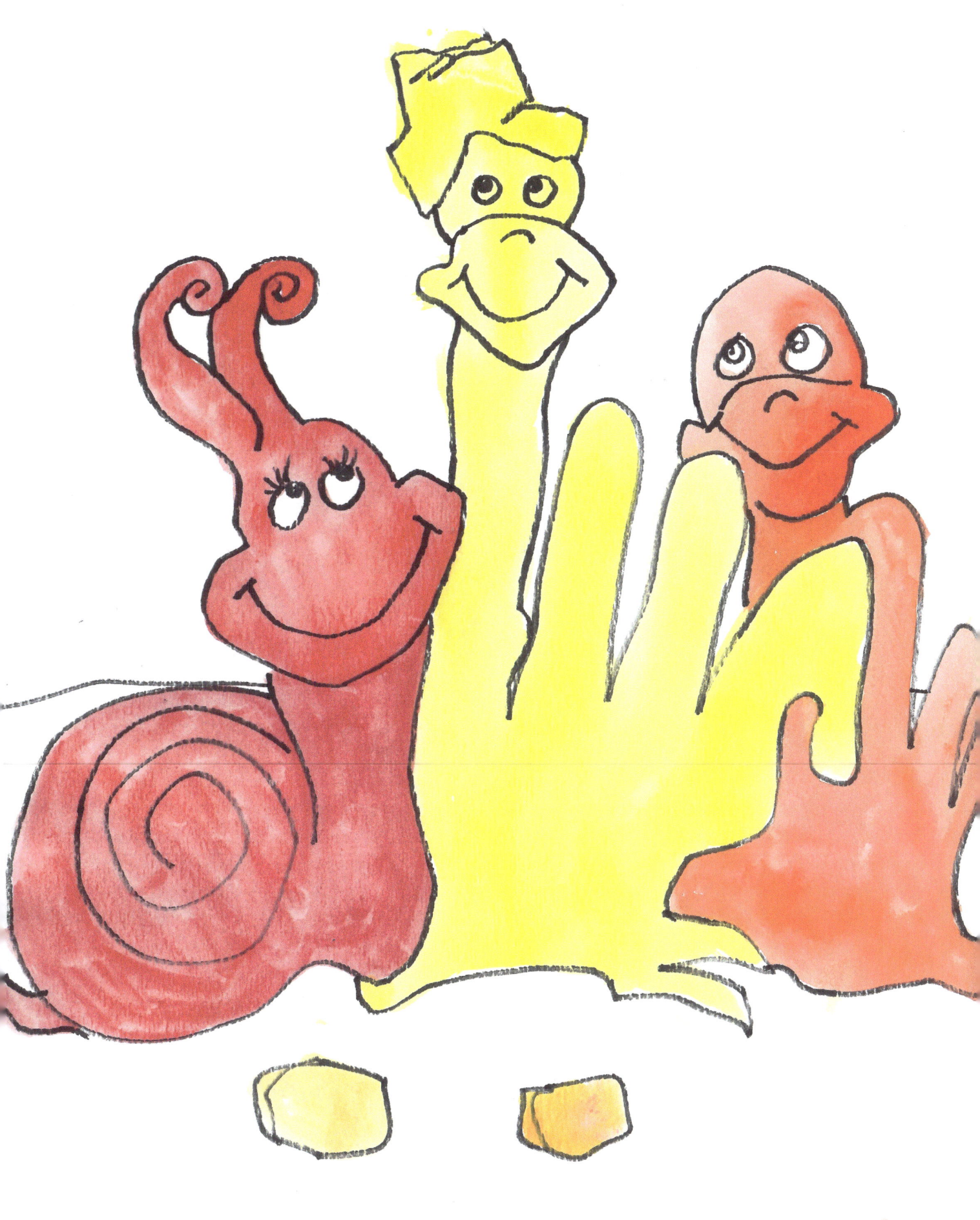

Then one day, Rosie had a surprise for Willie and Sammy. She had another child but this one looked more like her. She was a combination of both. A little bit of yellow but a whole lot more of red...but she was a kind of orange like Sammy. Welcome Sadie who is red orange! Didn't they all see red orange in the sunset?

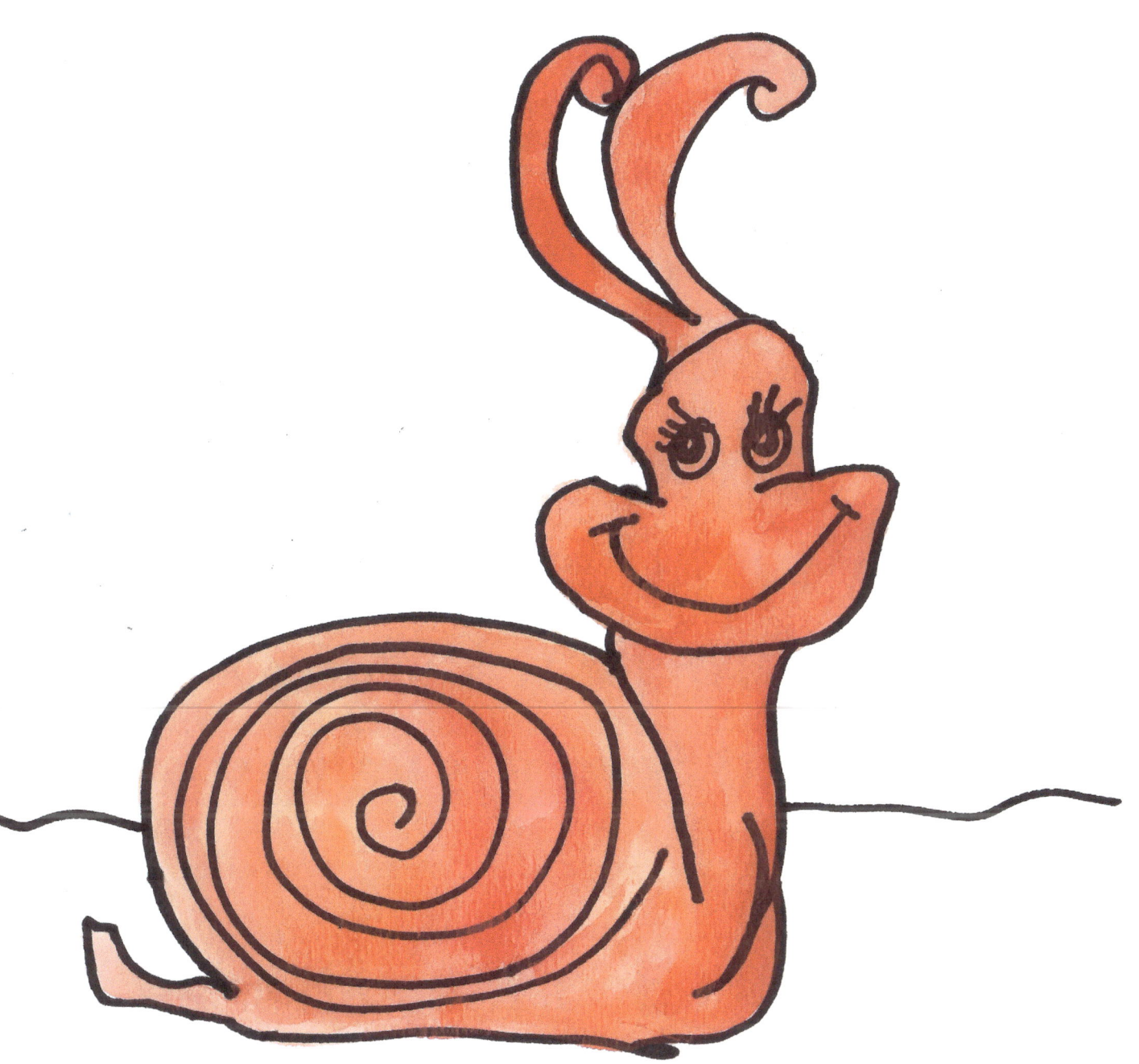

Willie and Rosie decided to add to their family. Meet Sonny! He is a beautiful mixture of Willie and Rosie but he looks more like Willie than Rosie. He looks a lot like Sammy too. They are both wiggly worms but Sammy is orange and Sonny is yellow orange!

But wait...hadn't they all seen yellow orange in the sunsets and sunrises on the beach?

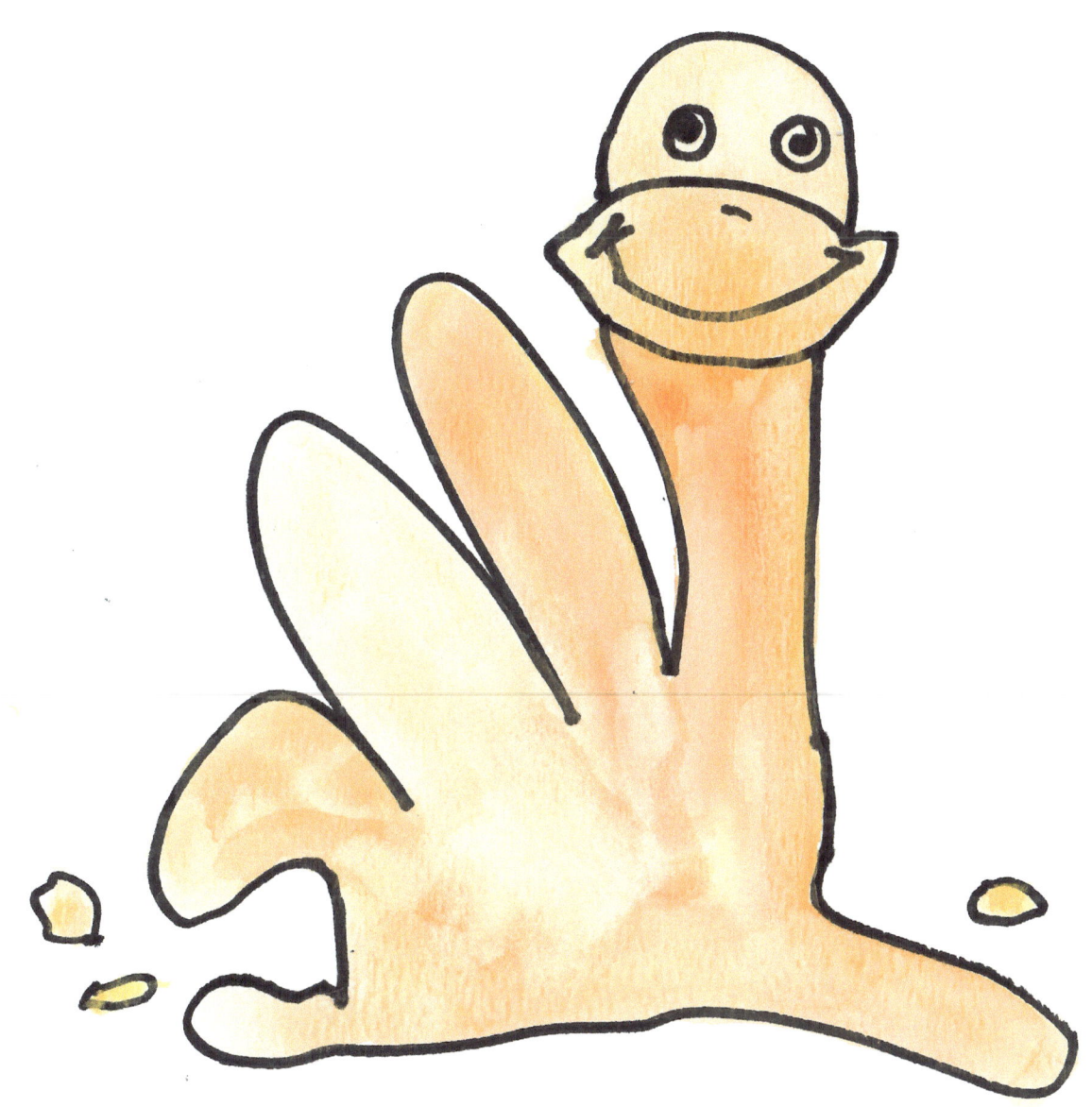

They were so very happy.

They called themselves the Orange Family!

Willie, the yellow dad

Rosie, the red mom

Sammy, the orange son

Sadie, the red orange daughter

Sonny, the yellow orange baby

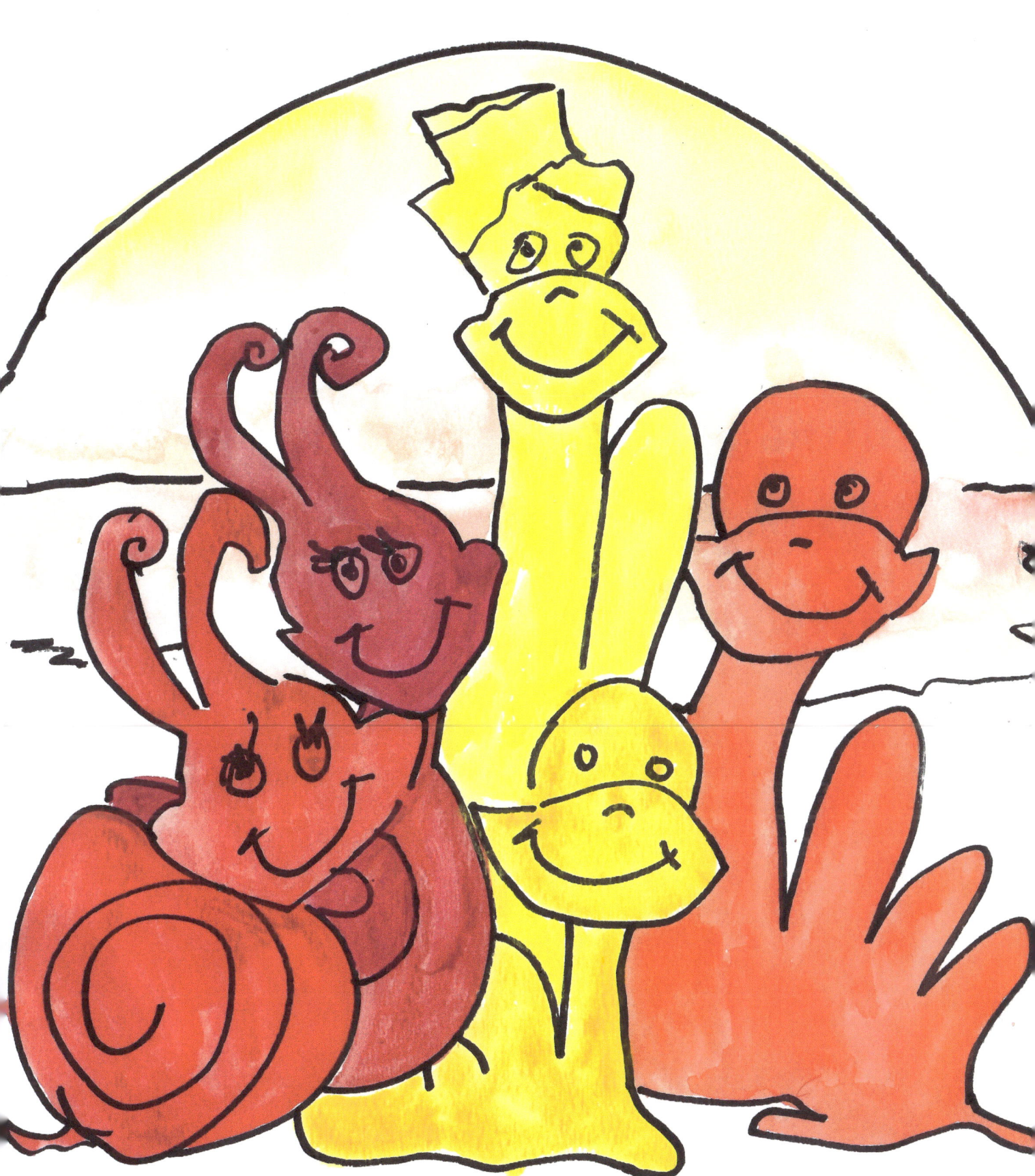

They walked the beach together and watched the sunset. Oh my! The sun was a big bright yellow, then red and turning red orange and orange and then yellow orange....

Just like them!

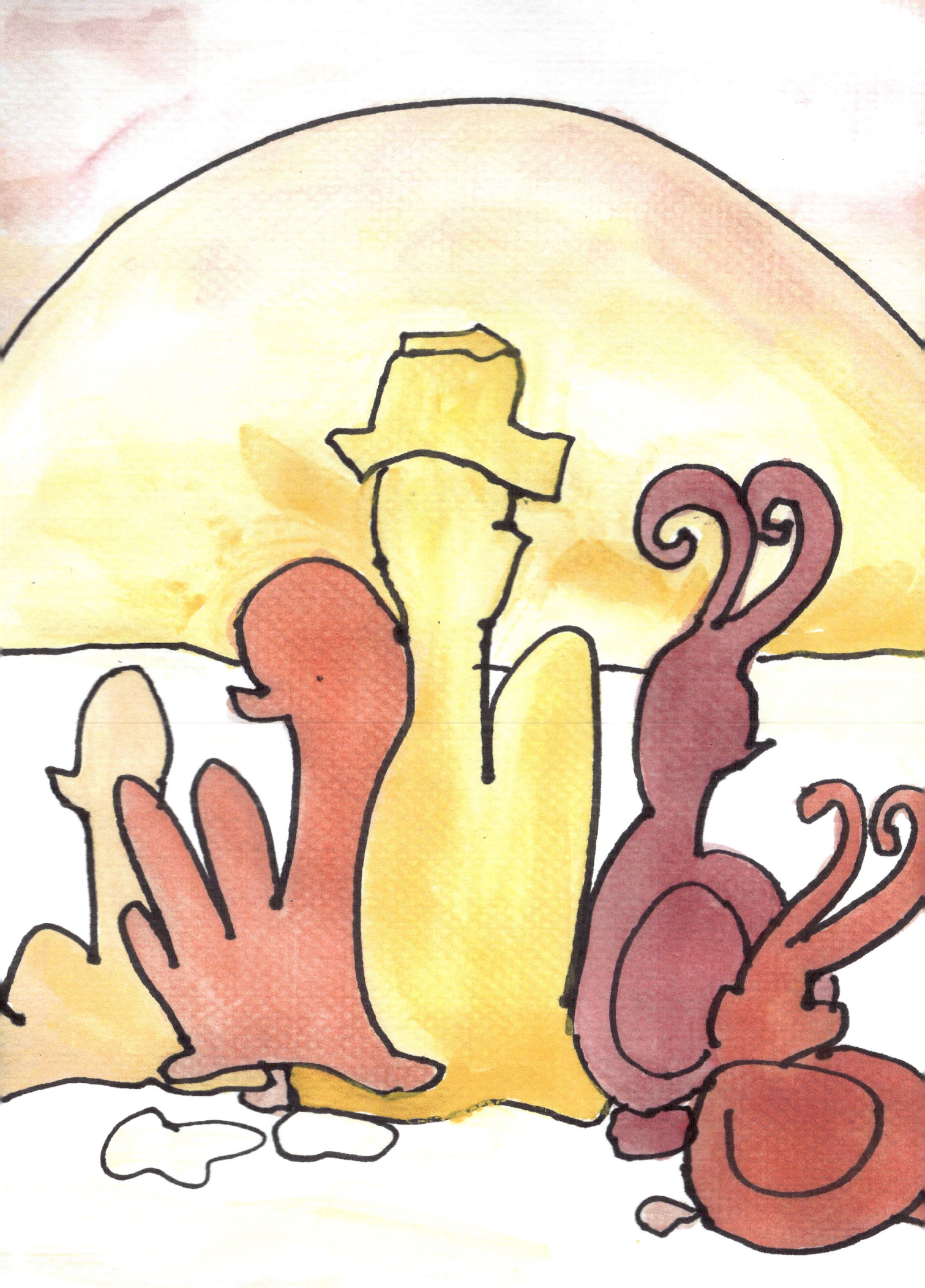

About the Author

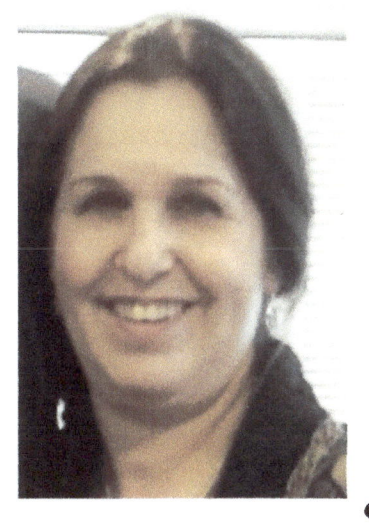

Joyce Brian is a retired art teacher who taught children of all ages...from pre-school through seniors in high school. She did this throughout her life as well as devoting time to being an artist.

Go to her website to view more of her artwork:

www.joycebrian.com

www.ingramcontent.com/pod-product-compliance
Lightning Source LLC
Chambersburg PA
CBHW051838210526
45473CB00005B/1934